BOOK ANALYSIS

Written by Natalia Torres Behar
Translated by Rebecca Neal

The Tunnel

BY ERNESTO SÁBATO

ERNESTO SÁBATO

ARGENTINIAN NOVELIST, ESSAYIST AND PAINTER

- **Born in Rojas (Argentina) in 1911.**
- **Died in Santo Lugares (Argentina) in 2011.**
- **Literary awards:**
  - Miguel de Cervantes Prize, 1984
  - Premio Gabriela Mistral, 1984
  - Jerusalem Prize, 1989
  - Menéndez Pelayo International Prize, 1997
- **Notable works:**
  - *The Tunnel* (1948), novel
  - *On Heroes and Tombs* (1961), novel
  - *The Writer in the Catastrophe of Our Time* (1963), essay
  - *The Angel of Darkness* (1974), novel

The Argentinian novelist, essayist and painter Ernesto Sábato was born in Rojas, Buenos Aires Province, to a family of Italian immigrants. He received a doctorate in physics from the National University of La Plata in 1937, and was subsequently awarded a grant to complete postdoctoral work at the Curie Laboratory in Paris. There, he met a number of members of the Surrealist movement and eventually decided to leave science to focus on writing. He returned to Argentina in 1940 and began teaching at the National University of Buenos Aires, but was forced to abandon his post for a year after publishing articles in which he attacked Juan Domingo Perón's (Argentinian general and politician, 1895-1974) regime. He used this time to work on his book *One and the Universe*, which was published in 1945. He went on to publish numerous essays and three novels (*The Tunnel*, 1948; *On Heroes and Tombs*, 1961; and *The Angel of Darkness*, 1974), which critics tend to consider a trilogy.

He opposed the National Reorganization Process (the military dictatorship that governed Argentina from 1976 to 1983), as can be seen in his newspaper columns and articles, and in books such as *The Sabato Case* (1956) and *The Other Face of Peronism* (1956). In 1984, he became the second Argentinian writer to receive the Miguel de Cervantes Prize, one of the most prestigious literary awards for Spanish-language writers (after Jorge Luis Borges, who was awarded the prize in 1979), and in the same year he received the Premio Gabriela Mistral, which is awarded by the Organization of American States. Sábato died in Santo Lugares, Argentina in 2011.

NUNCA MÁS

In 1984, Sábato was appointed president of the National Commission on the Disappearance of Persons (*Comisión Nacional sobre la Desaparición de Personas*, CONADEP), which produced a report entitled *Nunca Más* ("Never Again") on forced disappearances in Argentina during the National Reorganization Process. CONADEP was established by Raúl Alfonsín, the first democratically elected president after the end of the dictatorship, and its report in 1984 paved the way for the prosecution and sentencing of the leading figures of the military junta.

THE TUNNEL

AN INESCAPABLE LABYRINTH

- **Genre:** psychological novel/detective novel
- **Reference edition:** Sábato, E. (1988) *The Tunnel*. Trans. Sayers Peden, M. London: Penguin.
- **1ˢᵗ edition:** 1948
- **Themes:** isolation, miscommunication, loneliness

The Tunnel is widely recognised as one of the greatest Latin American novels of the 20th century. The first edition of the book was published in Buenos Aires during Juan Domino Perón's first stint as president (1946-1952) and immediately sold out. One year later, the French novelist and philosopher Albert Camus (1913-1960) wrote to Sábato to tell him that he had recommended that the French publishing house Gallimard release a French translation of the book. According to his diaries, the Nobel Prize-winning German author Thomas Mann (1875-1955) was also impressed by the novel.

The story displays many of the characteristics of detective fiction, is narrated in the first person, and recounts Juan Pablo Castel's motives for murdering María Iribarne in the hope that at least some readers will understand him. The reader is drawn into the narrator's labyrinthine subconscious and becomes acutely aware of his intensely bleak outlook on the world.

The Tunnel's protagonist is just one of the millions of anonymous inhabitants of the sprawling city of Buenos Aires, and the novel depicts his search for meaning and vain attempts to connect with other people.

SUMMARY

CONFESSION

The painter Juan Pablo Castel has murdered María Iribarne. He confesses to his crime in the opening lines of the novel and is aware that, since the trial that ended with him being sentenced to prison was a recent event, people probably still remember it. This is not his only confession: he also tells us that he is writing about why he killed the only person who could have saved him in "the faint hope that someone will understand me – *even if it is only one person*" (p. 5). As such, we know who committed the crime right from the beginning of the story and are taken on a journey to find out why he did it.

A LIFE-CHANGING ENCOUNTER

At the annual spring art show in Buenos Aires in 1946, Castel exhibited a painting called *Motherhood*. It contained a detail that most viewers and even critics missed, but that Castel feels is central to the work: a small window in the top left-hand corner, through which a woman on a beach looking out at the sea can be seen. Only one woman noticed it and lingered by the painting to admire it.

Castel developed an obsession with her and spent months scouring the city looking for her, fantasising all the while about potential opportunities to see her again and imagining how he would approach her. Over time, he finds out that the mysterious woman's name is María Iribarne, and when he finally sees her in the street, he approaches her and immediately asks her about the window in his painting.

To begin with, María pretends that she does not remember the scene, but when Castel is about to leave in disappointment, she admits that she knows exactly what he is talking about. He cannot stop thinking about her and wants to know if she thinks about him too. He gets his answer when he meets Maria's blind husband Allende one day while Maria is out of town at the estancia (a term used in Argentina to refer to a large cattle ranch) and Allende passes on a letter addressed to him from Maria. Castel is confused by the letter's content and by the fact that María is married, and develops his own theory to make sense of the situation and explain why she never mentioned her husband before. After María returns to Buenos Aires, she and Castel start seeing one another regularly.

LOVE AND OBSESSION

Castel and María's relationship remains steady for over a month. He is so happy to have found someone to pull him out of his solitude that his bleak outlook on the world becomes brighter, but his jealousy and incessant questions make life difficult for both of them. As he interrogates María about her private life, her relationships and her beliefs, he sinks deeper and deeper into despair. His awareness of the sudden, unpredictable changes in his behaviour and his distress at the slow demise of his relationship drive him to drown his sorrows in alcohol and sleep with prostitutes. He then dreams that he has been transformed into a monstrous bird and that nobody realises that he is screeching when he tries to talk. He calls María in despair, and she eventually invites him to the estancia.

DOUBT AND DEATH

At the estancia, Castel is greeted by Allende's cousins Hunter and Mimí, who ask him about his painting. When María finally appears, they go for a walk on the beach together. As they stand by the sea in silence, María confesses that the scene in the painting also made her realise that they had a connection, but Castel's happiness at this news is short-lived as he becomes convinced that there is something between María and Hunter.

Castel then returns to Buenos Aires and falls back into his old habits of drinking to excess, getting into fights and frequenting prostitutes. He is on the verge of a total breakdown, and writes an aggressive letter to María about his suspicions. Although he regrets sending the letter, he calls her at the estancia and threatens to kill himself if she does not come and see him in Buenos Aires. She agrees to return, but then does not show up to their meeting because she urgently needs to go back to the estancia. This pushes Castel over the edge: he follows her there, and although he remembers all the good times they shared, he now feels very distant from her. After he sees her with Hunter, he flies into a jealous rage, goes up onto the balcony and kills her. When he returns to Buenos Aires, Castel tells Allende that María was having an affair with him and, he suspects, with Hunter too. Allende chases Castel while shouting repeatedly that he is a "fool" (p. 138). Castel then hands himself in to the police, and right at the end of the novel we learn that Allende has committed suicide.

CHARACTER STUDY

JUAN PABLO CASTEL

The 38-year-old painter Juan Pablo Castel is the novel's narrator and protagonist. He is highly intelligent, sensitive, cynical, self-critical and misanthropic. He is particularly contemptuous of the superficiality, arrogance and pettiness of the elites, who use meaningless jargon to impress other people and bolster their false sense of superiority. He wants to establish meaningful connections and find someone who understands him, but whether he wants to or not, he ends up torturing himself by obsessing over minor details.

Although he is extremely rational and intellectually sophisticated, he lacks emotional depth, which leaves him trapped in his own mind and unable to connect with other people. Some critics have interpreted his surname, which is an archaic form of "castle", as a reflection of the way he walls himself up in the fortress of his mind. His encounter with María Iribarne changes his life, encourages him to adopt a new style of painting and forces him to struggle against his own nature to communicate and fully connect with her.

MARÍA IRIBARNE

María is a young brown-haired woman who looks as if she cannot be more than 26 years old. She is married to Allende, whom she greatly admires, and Castel sees her as a mysterious figure. The fact that she is drawn to the window in Castel's painting *Motherhood* creates a bond between them, and he sees her as a soulmate who understands and shares his loneliness.

However, María never lets him see into the depths of her soul, and the loneliness that apparently unites them is not as straightforward as it may seem. Indeed, one of the biggest differences between Castel and María is that she seems to be capable of fitting in and relating to the people around her. Having said that, she seems more energetic and at home at the estancia that Allende's cousin Hunter runs, and frequently feels the need to escape there.

ALLENDE

Allende is María's husband. He is tall, thin and blind and contrasts with Castel, both because of his relationship with María, which mystifies and obsesses Castel, and because he seems to be at peace with the world around him. His physical blindness is juxtaposed with Castel's emotional blindness, which prevents him from looking beyond his suspicions about María and seeing her for who she really is. Allende sees more clearly and more deeply than Castel, and seems to truly understand María. She cares about him a lot and greatly admires him, which infuriates Castel.

HUNTER

Hunter is Allende's cousin. He is tall, slim and tanned, and tends to avoid eye contact. He works as an architect and is currently single, although Castel cannot remember if this is because he is unmarried, divorced or widowed. He is described as cynical, a womaniser, superficial, petty, apathetic and hypocritical. He runs the estancia that María often goes to, and Castel is convinced that they are lovers, although the true nature of their relationship is never made clear.

MIMÍ

Mimí is malicious, short-sighted, frivolous and superficial. Castel meets her when he goes to visit María at the estancia. She has some French ancestry, which she uses as a justification for her pedantry. She often uses French words in every-day conversation, and even Hunter makes fun of her for this.

ANALYSIS

Structure and genre

The Tunnel comprises 39 short chapters. Although there are no clear structural divisions, one of the narrator's comments towards the start of the novel allows us to identify the distinct stages of the story. At the start of the third chapter, he says "Everyone knows that I killed María Iribarne Hunter. But no one knows how I met her, exactly what our relationship was, or why I came to believe I had to kill her" (p. 6). This allows us to divide the narrative into three parts: Castel's meeting with María, his relationship with her and his desire to kill her. Adding in the initial chapters in which he introduces himself gives us a total of four parts. The story is shaped by the techniques of both the psychological novel and the detective novel.

The psychological novel

Techniques from the psychological novel are used to construct Castel's character and to depict his inner conflict and his transformation over the course of the story, which is driven by external factors. The narrative does not aim to tell us what happened, as we know this from the beginning, but rather why it happened and what drove Castel to commit his crime. This explains why Sábato uses internal monologues and stream of consciousness to reveal his protagonist's thoughts and irrational ideas.

The detective novel

Detective novels are typically structured around a key event, usually a crime, and generally focus on the investigation into this crime. However, whereas the structure of traditional detective novels is shaped by the crime, the investigation to uncover the criminal's identity and mounting intrigue, *The Tunnel* takes an original approach. The narrator begins telling the story at the end, and the mystery is not who the victim or the criminal was, but rather why the criminal committed their crime. The novel therefore blends the genres of psychological and detective fiction, since the mystery is not unravelled by a detective relying on specific facts, but instead has a significant psychological dimension: the narrative focuses on the motives behind the crime and the thoughts, ideas and obsessions that drove Castel to kill María.

Style and language

Perhaps the most immediately obvious stylistic feature of *The Tunnel* is the orality of the narrative. The novel's narration, which is from the protagonist's perspective, takes the form of a stream of consciousness in which events are not recounted in chronological order and time seems to speed up or slow down depending on the episode being discussed. This is interspersed with asides featuring explicit dialogue, and the overall effect is that we learn more about the character from his thoughts than from his actions and become aware of all the nuances and contradictions of his personality.

Furthermore, one of the modifications introduced when the Spanish text was revised in 1971 serves to accentuate its oral dimension. The verb form "tú" (meaning "you") was replaced by "vos", which has the same meaning but is far more common in Argentinian speech, regardless of the social status of the speaker. This is a significant alteration, and serves to make the narrative more authentic and natural, given that its characters are Argentinian and would be more likely to speak in this way. In a private letter, Sábato confirmed that the change was his idea and was motivated his desire to reflect the observations about language that he had made in his essays in his novels.

THEMES

Isolation and loneliness

The narrator's profound loneliness can be seen from the beginning of the novel thanks to the confessional style he uses to tell his story. The reader is trapped in Castel's mind, as we only have access to his point of view. The author uses various means to signify his growing isolation:

- **Natural imagery** which reinforces the sense that he is lonely and isolated (the sea, a dark, turbulent river, desert islands, desolate landscapes, a dark cave).

- **Symbolic dreams** which provide a link between the novel's theme and structure, as they reinforce the protagonist's profound isolation and solitude. In his first dream, Castel visits an old house that he has longed to return to since he was a child, but in spite of the location's familiarity, he feels lost and is afraid that he will be attacked by hidden enemies. When he feels that he is rediscovering the ability to love, he concludes that the house represents María. The dream means that when we are feeling lonely, we try to connect with other people through love, but at the same time we are afraid of the risks that this entails, such as misunderstandings and miscommunications.

Castel's loneliness is self-inflicted and entirely a result of his negative outlook on life. Moreover, as we can see from his opinions on humanity, his personality pushes him further into isolation: he does not see people as individuals, but rather as members of categories or groups. Even when he has to deal with individuals, he reacts to others with fear and suspicion, especially given that he tends to see ulterior motives in everything that other people say or do.

The impossibility of effective communication

Relatedly, we can say that *The Tunnel* is about the problems of human communication, or rather the lack thereof. Sábato repeatedly shows us that communication is impossible: for example, while he uses natural imagery to symbolise loneliness, he depicts man-made structures such as walls, rooms, a building, a prison cell and, most significantly, the tunnel, as a way of signifying the impossibility of communicating with other people. When Castel knows that he has lost María forever, he compares their lives to dark tunnels which run parallel to one another and seem to meet through the window in his painting. Like the main character in Fyodor Dostoyevsky's (Russian author, 1821-1881) novella *Notes from Underground* (1864), Castel has never emerged from his tunnel to truly live his life.

The use of symbolic dreams is also linked to this theme. In his second dream, Castel has been invited to a house where the host turns him into a monstrous bird. This clear nod to Franz Kafka (German-language novelist, 1883-1924) has an unexpected result, as the other people present fail to notice his metamorphosis, and his attempts to inform them of it results in a screech that they hear as his normal voice. This dream comes just before the climax of Castel's fight with María, is followed by his certainty that she has deceived him, and has a clear meaning: after finally managing to connect with other people, Castel feels that he has been lied to, but has no way of communicating this.

FURTHER REFLECTION

SOME QUESTIONS TO THINK ABOUT...

- Why does Castel kill María? Use examples from the text to support your answer.
- Does Castel change over the course of the novel? Justify your answer using examples.
- What role do the novel's secondary characters play in Castel and María's story?
- What do you think Castel's painting *Motherhood* looks like? Why do you think that nobody noticed the window in the corner?
- What role does the city of Buenos Aires play in the novel's development?
- Why does Allende shout "fool" (p. 138) at Castel when he says that he and Hunter were both María's lovers?
- What is the significance of the italics in the following extract from the novel? "[...] [T]he whole story of the passageways was my own ridiculous invention, and that *after all there was only one tunnel, dark and solitary: mine,*

the tunnel I which had spent my childhood, my youth, my entire life. And in one of those transparent sections of the stone wall I had seen this girl and had naïvely believed that she was moving in a tunnel parallel to mine, when in fact she belonged to the wide world, the unbounded world of those who did not live in tunnel" (p. 133).

- *The Tunnel* has been adapted for television and the cinema on multiple occasions, and Sábato adapted the script himself for one of these adaptations. Choose one adaptation and highlight the main differences between it and the novel. How are the characters depicted? Which themes are emphasised?

We want to hear from you!
Leave a comment on your online library
and share your favourite books on social media!

FURTHER READING

REFERENCE EDITION

- Sábato, E. (1988) *The Tunnel*. Trans. Sayers Peden, M. London: Penguin.

REFERENCE STUDIES

- Foster, D. W. (1971) Tú y vos en "El túnel" de Ernesto Sábato. *Hispania.* 54(2), pp. 354-355. [Online]. [Accessed 27 February 2018]. Available from: <http://www.jstor.org/stable/337802>
- Gibbs, B. J. (1965) "El Túnel": Portrayal of Isolation. *Hispania.* 48(3), pp. 429-436. [Online]. [Accessed 27 February 2018]. Available from: <http://www.jstor.org/stable/336464>
- Meehan, T. C. (1968) Ernesto Sábato's Sexual Metaphysics: Theme and Form in El túnel. *MLN.* 83(2), pp. 226-252. [Online]. [Accessed 27 February 2018]. Available from: <http://www.jstor.org/stable/2908197>
- Ortega, J. (1983) Las tres obsesiones de Sábato. *Cuadernos Hispanoamericanos.* Issues 391-393, pp. 125-151. [Online]. [Accessed 27 February 2018]. Available from: <http://www.cervantesvirtual.

com/nd/ark:/59851/bmcxp7k5>

- Sauter, S. (2004) *Estudio introductorio de* El túnel *de Ernesto Sábato*. Bogotá: Editorial Planeta.

RECOMMENDED READING

- Kafka, F. (2015) *Metamorphosis and Other Stories*. Trans. Hofmann, M. London: Penguin.

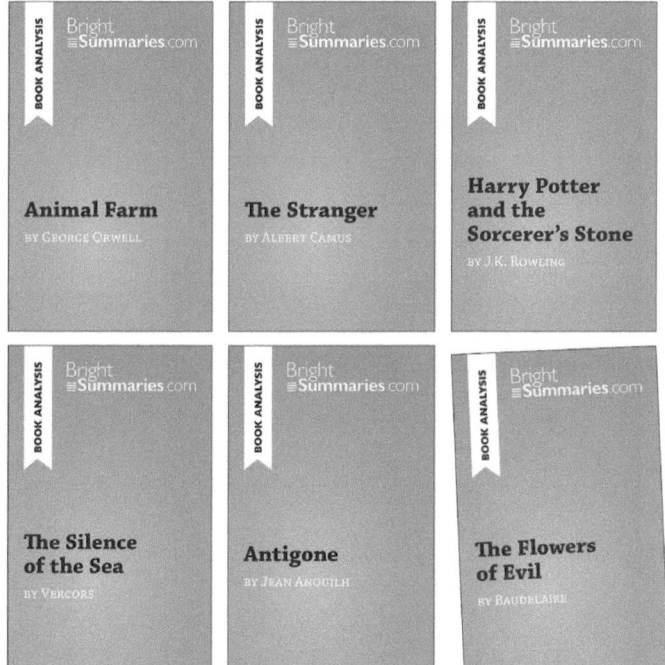

www.brightsummaries.com

Ebook EAN: 9782808001762

Paperback EAN: 9782808008778

Legal Deposit: D/2018/12603/193

Cover: © Primento

Digital conception by Primento, the digital partner of publishers.